METHODISM'S MESSAGE
IN MODERN TERMS

METHODISM'S MESSAGE
IN MODERN TERMS

BY

H. MORTIMER SINFIELD

THE EPWORTH PRESS
(EDGAR C. BARTON)
25–35 City Road, London, E.C.1

This book is produced in complete conformity
with the authorized economy standards

Made in Great Britain

TO
MY WIFE

CONTENTS

NOTE

Special permission has been received and fees paid for the quotations from the poems of G. A. Studdert Kennedy, published by Hodder and Stoughton, Ltd.

Come, O Thou that hast the seven stars in Thy right hand, . . . perfect and accomplish Thy glorious acts . . . and as Thou didst dignify our Father's days with many revelations above all the foregoing ages since Thou tookest the Flesh; so Thou canst vouchsafe to us, though unworthy, as large a portion of Thy Spirit as Thou pleasest. . . . Seeing the power of Thy Grace is not passed away with the primitive times as fond and foolish men imagine, but Thy Kingdom is now at hand, and Thou standing at the door. —MILTON.

FOREWORD

Keen observers have noticed what appear to be two contradictory tendencies in modern religious life. There is a deepening desire for Church reunion and there is a renewal of stress upon denominational distinctiveness. Both! Both together! People completely committed to one or other of these movements sometimes deny the one they oppose, but those who view the scene with detachment are in no doubt that both are there.

Nor are they as contradictory as they first appear.

When the desire for Church reunion becomes so passionate that it blurs honest differences and is eager to strip away from the denominations every shred of distinctiveness, striving all the time for some deliberately vague formula which will tie inconsistencies together by ambiguities, the cause of true religion is harmed. It would be better to remind 'the man in the street' that people lived before him and honestly differed from one another, than to try and win his tepid interest in religion by faking a unity which is not really there.

Moreover, true Catholicism is a *rich* thing. It will include whatever men have found precious in their pilgrimage with God. For any Communion to jettison some important part of its heritage in the mistaken notion that it will hasten real reunion is to be unworthy of its spiritual past.

There is a deep synthesis beyond this shallow contradiction. The God-given longing for reunion can live with a true regard for one's denominational distinctiveness. To cherish what one has found dear and bring it as a contribution to the Whole is not to deny the worth of things which have nourished the souls of other people, but rather to have patience with the patience of God and trust Him

B

to give the experience which knits us together, even while our explanations may keep us apart.

It is on that background that this book should be read. The denominational distinctiveness of Methodism is dear to the author. Methodism is not merely the Church of his birth, but the Church of his choice. He denies nobody else's experience: he witnesses to his own. Simple language and homely illustration mark his pages. It is not a book for theological scholars, but it will not offend them. They will be the first to see that he is aiming at the hard task of putting deep things in plain words. He is glad to be—in the way the French might use the word—a 'vulgarizer': to stand between the doctors of the Church and the mass of the people . . . and interpret.

It is a high calling.

I commend his book.

W. E. SANGSTER

THE CENTRAL HALL
WESTMINSTER, S.W.1

PREFACE

Some years ago a ministerial colleague expressed the opinion that the Methodism to which we both belonged was 'done'. It had fulfilled its purpose and had exhausted itself in the process, and he averred we should both live to see its disappearance.

The writer of this little book cannot hold such views. He does not think Methodism has yet fulfilled its purpose, nor does he consider its end imminent. On the contrary, he firmly believes that the denomination which he has the honour of serving as a minister, still has a powerful and needed message to proclaim, and still has an important work to do—a work which perhaps no other denomination can do, for Methodism has not only a unique history, but also a unique equipment.

This little book is offered to the public, then, in the belief that our message is still pertinent, and in the hope that its pages will help to make that message clear and convincing to those who have neither time nor inclination to probe into the more academic literature of Methodism. There are many, we find—even among those who proudly wear the label 'Methodist', who know surprisingly little about her history, and even less about her distinctive emphases. Perhaps a little book like this will awaken their interest in both.

It is especially hoped that the book will be helpful to young people, and the basis of further study and discussion in Groups, Classes, Study Circles, and the like. For this purpose a list of ten interesting and very readable books is furnished at the back of the book as a guide for further study. These books are selected because, with the exception of *Wesley's Sermons*, they are all easy to read, interesting, and accurate. The *Sermons* will demand a little more concentration, but fully repay such effort.

As stated in the Prologue, the chapters which follow were originally offered to my congregation as a series of sermons, and when so delivered it was not contemplated that they would be printed. There are consequently defects in the book which would perhaps not have occurred had it been prepared specifically for the Press. The sermons were preached during the mid-war years when our people were tired in body, anxious in mind, and jaded in spirit, and when they found it difficult to sustain interest for long in carefully worked-out argument. Consequently, my aim was to offer profound truths in the simplest and most interesting ways I could devise.

I should like to express my very warm gratitude to my friend Dr. W. E. Sangster for writing the Foreword, and for valued advice and suggestions, and also to Miss Gwen Tanswell, who has helped me so willingly in the typing of the manuscript and a score of other ways, and last but not least, my wife, who not only offered invaluable help by reading manuscript and proofs, but who also by her devotion, patience, and understanding has made it possible in the midst of these war days to produce this bit of extra work.

H. M. S.

WOLVERHAMPTON
February 1945

PROLOGUE

I WAS sitting in a beautiful drawing-room conversing one afternoon with a lady. 'I am a member of the Church of England,' she was saying, and then, half apologetically, she added: 'But I don't think it really matters much what you believe, do you?'

I smiled. 'I don't think I quite know what you mean,' I said. 'Do you really mean that you don't think it matters what one believes? We Methodists think it matters a great deal. You see, there are certain central doctrines that we think are of supreme importance. It was the emphasis of these by John Wesley that called Methodism into being; and it is the continued belief in their supreme importance which we Methodists think justifies the continuance of our Church as a separate denomination.'

My hostess looked puzzled, and, after gazing into the fire for a moment or two, said somewhat reflectively: 'Oh! I see ——' and then: 'What are those central doctrines that you think are so supremely important?'

It was an attempt to answer that question which prompted me to preach some little time ago a series of sermons on 'The Distinctive Doctrines of Methodism'. I had only a little while earlier been asked for a book of a popular nature suitable for putting into the hands of inquiring adolescents on the distinctive emphases of our denomination; and so, with these two incidents in mind, I set to work to try to offer my congregation—which is composed of people of varied denominations—a *popular* statement of the doctrines which we Methodists consider to be of tremendous importance.

I have since slightly altered these sermons ready for print and offer them here in this little book, in the hope that others who wish to know what Methodism's central emphases are may be helped.

I have deliberately avoided the use of technical terms wherever possible, and endeavoured to express profound truths in the simplest possible way, ever striving to make my theme as interesting as I can by a liberal use of illustrations.

I am aware that many of my readers will be neither trained thinkers nor extensive readers. Specialized callings in these days demand the careful and extensive study of one's own particular work and leave little time for other studies; and many people, I am fully aware, like—when they have leisure to take up a book—to find one both interesting and easy to follow. To satisfy their need has been my aim.

When David slew Goliath, he selected from the stream five smooth stones. There is a Goliath to be slain to-day. It is the 'Goliath' of irreligion; and I believe that the best weapons of attack are the five smooth stones of Methodism's central emphases, namely: (1) 'Salvation by faith', (2) 'Assurance', (3) 'Holiness', (4) 'The belief in the universality of God's grace', and (5) 'The inevitability of Judgement'.

I shall endeavour in the chapters that follow to consider each of these emphases in turn; and first we will consider 'Salvation by faith'. Wesley's famous sermon on this, preached in the Church of St. Mary the Virgin, Oxford, was 'Methodism's Manifesto'.

CHAPTER I

METHODISM'S MANIFESTO—
SALVATION BY FAITH

For by grace are ye saved through faith; and that not of yourselves: it is the gift of God.
EPHESIANS ii. 8.

IT is a hot June afternoon, and as the clock in the ancient 'Tom Tower' of Oxford chimes the hour, a stately procession enters the old church of St. Mary the Virgin. The Squire Bedel heads the column carrying the insignia of the Vice-Chancellor. After him comes the Vice-Chancellor himself, resplendent in his robes of office; and following him the preacher for the day, arrayed in full canonicals. Then come the Proctors, and the Doctors of Divinity—arrayed in scarlet glory—bringing up the rear.

The occasion is one of the annual services when all doctors, masters, graduates, and scholars are desired to attend, and when the preachers are selected from the various colleges in turn.

The preacher for this day is one, John Wesley—Master of Arts and Fellow of Lincoln College. He is thirty-five years of age, of medium height, and calm in manner.

As the procession enters the church the vast congregation rises, and when the centre of the church is reached, the Vice-Chancellor bows to the preacher and moves to his throne, while Wesley ascends the pulpit opposite. A hymn is sung, a 'bidding-prayer' is offered, and then the text is announced.

In a clear, steady voice Wesley reads out Paul's great words, 'By grace are ye saved through faith', and as he proceeds with his sermon an unusual hush is felt in the ancient sanctuary.

Only eighteen days previously Wesley's 'heart' had been

'strangely warmed' in that epoch-making experience in Aldersgate Street; and as he preaches, every word seems to glow with reality, and every sentence to throb with earnestness. Indeed, his words ring out before that solemn assembly like a great manifesto. They are indeed, the manifesto of a Methodism-to-be!

That ancient church of the Blessed Virgin Mary on Oxford's High Street has reverberated with many epoch-making utterances. It was here that the brave Cranmer 'witnessed a good confession' before going out to the stake near Balliol. It was here that Newman and Pusey preached the sermons which initiated the 'Oxford Movement' in the nineteenth century; but, as Dr. Sugden, the great Methodist scholar has said: 'Never have its ancient walls re-echoed words of more far-reaching importance in the history of religion than when on this day Wesley blew the first trumpet-call of the Evangelical Revival.'[1]

That trumpet call was: '*For by grace are ye saved through faith; and that not of yourselves: it is the gift of God.*' That, indeed, was the text on which Methodism was launched! It was to early Methodism what a slipway is to a life-boat. Down the slipway, the life-boat of Methodism sped to its work of rescue and redemption.

Do we still believe its truths—or have we outgrown them? While we have never actually read the obituary notice of the text and its implied doctrines, we have, however, for some time had an uncomfortable suspicion that the text and its doctrines have long ago been given a secret burial! If that be so, our aim in this chapter is to disinter it, and, by God's grace, make the dead words live again.

We propose to consider three things:

(1) Salvation.
(2) Grace.
(3) Faith.

[1] Sugden, *Standard Sermons of John Wesley*, vol. I, p. 36.

Salvation, we suggest, is our primary *need*;

Grace is God's free offer; and

Faith is our method of responding to that offer. Let us consider each in turn.

I. SALVATION

Salvation is our Primary Need! But is it? Doesn't our modern respectability cancel out such a need? The author has been in a slum attic where the only furniture was an upturned box serving as a table, and where, in indescribable filth and wretchedness, a drunkard and his family lived in squalid poverty. Obviously, people like that need *saving*. Their need is as great and obvious as 'the heathen in his blindness'. But surely we are different from wretches like that! We are respectable and respected citizens—doesn't the very respectability cancel out our need of salvation?

The Bible doesn't think so! It has a disconcerting habit of facing facts—not as they *appear*—but as they really *are*. Appearances can be very deceptive. Every schoolmaster knows that the boy with the innocent look and saintly face can be the most mischievous little rascal in the class. The Bible isn't deceived by the outward—it gets right down to the inward—and it claims that right at the heart of human nature there is cardiac weakness—heart disease! It is the disease of a tainted nature. 'There is none righteous, no not one.'

We know, of course, that there is something wonderful in the human heart. You see it in the heroism and unselfishness which shines out with such radiant splendour in war days. And the Bible admits this—man is created in God's image, it says. But somehow, the image has got marred—there is an ugly smear across the loveliness—the smear of innate sin. Studdert Kennedy expressed it graphically in his dialect poem:

> There's nothing in man that's perfect,
> And nothin' that's all complete,
> 'E's nobutt a big beginning
> From 'is 'ead to the soles of 'is feet;
> There's summat as draws 'im uppards,
> And summat as drags 'im dahn,
> And the consikence is 'e wobbles
> 'Twixt muck and a golden crown.[1]

You are conscious of it, reader, aren't you? If you aren't then your sin has drugged your conscience so that it has become insensitive. Every man who really tries knows how appallingly hard is the road upward, and the more sincerely men try, the more they become conscious of failure: 'they who fain would serve Thee best, are conscious most of wrong within.'

There is in every heart:

> That underworld where lust and lies,
>   Like vermin crawl and creep,
> Across my vision and my prayers
>   Whence sordid passions leap.
>
> To slay the very thing I love,
> To crucify my Lord,
> And force me spit my sins upon,
>   The face my soul adored.[2]

Yes, there is no doubt about our need—*we all of us need salvation*.

But how? That is the problem. Indeed, it has been humanity's problem all the way through history. Every chapter of history tells the story of man's attempt to save himself—his burnt offerings, his ceremonial ablutions, his self-inflicted ordeals, his penances, his disciplines—but none of them avails. Man can no more save himself from sin than he can lift himself by pulling at his own boot-laces.

[1] *G. A. Studdert Kennedy, by His Friends*, p. 133 (Hodder & Stoughton).
[2] G. A. Studdert Kennedy, *Food for the Fed-up.* p. 157.

It was this realization that brought about the Reformation under Martin Luther. You probably remember the story of his terrible search for Salvation. How he fasted, did penance, prayed, meditated, and went on pilgrimage. Then they told him of the *Scala Santa*—the sacred stairway in the ancient city of Rome. If, he was told, he ascended these stairs, which tradition claimed had been trodden by the Saviour's feet, on his knees, praying at each step and kissing it as he went, he would cleanse his soul and find favour with God. To the Holy City, therefore, he went in an ecstasy of hope, but soon the futility and absurdity of it depressed his soul. Then as he pursued his great purpose, a text shot into his mind. 'The just shall live by faith.' The truth dawned. It wasn't anything he could do! All that had to be done *had already been done* by Christ—it was given in grace—all he must do is *accept*. So began the Reformation!

Yes, Salvation is our primary need. That is our first point.

But how are we saved? *By grace!*

2. GRACE

Grace means unmerited favour and love. It is easier to illustrate than define. Here is an incident which illustrates it: In a town where I ministered a short while ago, a Roman priest appeared in the police court to plead for a man who had wronged him. The man stole and drank four and a half bottles of Communion wine, and then stole £12 odd worth of the priest's possessions. But, instead of desiring the man's punishment, the priest had gone to court and pleaded for the man, and assured the court that if a fine was necessary, he would pay it. *That was grace!* Free, unmerited favour.

God offers salvation as a gift—an unmerited favour. His offer is twofold. It is an offer of pardon and power.

The pardon was manifest in the Cross. The power in the Resurrection.

Pardon!

This is the meaning of the Cross. It is God's assurance of forgiveness. I have seen it stated that in the Old Testament days, if a man had fallen badly into debt and was what we would call bankrupt, it was the custom to inscribe his financial liabilities on a parchment and nail it in a public place for all to see. But sometimes a friend, seeing the grim document, would fold over the parchment and inscribe his own name across the back. That meant that he had taken all the liabilities unto himself, he would pay the debts. Then the poor bankrupt's honour was saved and his burden lifted.[1] That is what Jesus did on the Cross. He cancelled the debt—He lifted the burden. The Cross manifests God's grace freeing us from the guilt of sin.

Grace also means *power!*

Paul is always writing of power; it is a favourite word. He prays in the Epistles that his readers may understand the 'surpassing greatness of His power'. How tragically we seem to have missed the significance of this in our modern Christianity. How ineffectual we often are. How timid and sceptical we are. How little we venture—personally and collectively. How little we dare because we know not the power. Scepticism seems to have insulated our souls. We fail to attempt great things *for* God because we fail to expect great things *from* God. But this is part of the meaning of Grace—an offer of power, the power of the risen Christ.

It is a power that transforms.

When Robert Browning was visiting Florence, he picked up one day on a second-hand bookstall a faded pamphlet for an absurdly small sum. It was a soiled and

[1] I am indebted for this illustration to the Rev. Leslie D. Weatherhead who quotes it in a footnote on p. 83 of *This is the Victory*.

dust-covered document, and it contained a sordid story. But Browning passed the story through his own wonderful brain, purified it, and out of the sordid tale produced his master poem, *The Ring and the Book*. Out of the soiled and sordid he brought beauty and perfection. This is what God's grace—grace as power—does for man.

3. FAITH

Salvation is our need. It is offered by Grace. It is accepted by Faith.

Faith is the reaching out of a hand to receive. Faith is to the Christian what the trolley-bus arm is to the trolley-bus—it is the lifting up of an expectant arm to receive the enabling power.

Now, Saving Faith is twofold. It is partly intellectual, partly volitional. Its intellectual side is the acceptance by the *mind*, of the truth of the Gospel. Its volitional side is the action of the *will* in venturing on that truth.

Again illustration is better than definition. Here is a story which illustrates both these aspects. When I was a boy, my father took my sister and I one day to see over a battleship which was moored a few miles off the coast of my home town. All afternoon we wandered over the wonderful floating fortress. Slowly but surely, however, we began to realize that the floors were not always at the same angle, and eventually we were told that a rough sea had developed and it was unsafe to return to the land (most of us had come out to the battleship by pinnaces), so we were told we'd better prepare to stay on board overnight!

Presently, however, a mine-sweeper drew up alongside. Like a cork, she bobbed about by the great ship's side— now twenty feet below us, now deck level, now yards out from the gunwale, now bumping alarmingly against the vessel's steel side. Several sailors decided to board her.

Standing on the gunwale, holding fast to the rails, they waited an opportune moment, and when the smaller craft was on the ascent they sprang aboard and were caught by the sweeper's crew as their boat dropped with the descending wave. Then they asked if any civilian would care to run the risk. 'Yes,' piped a childish voice: it was my little sister! Two sailors held her tightly as she stood on the ship's edge. 'Now,' they instructed, 'when we say go, you jump!' Down went the minesweeper, bumping and clanging against the battleship's side. 'Now,' they cried. 'Up she comes. Ready, steady——' Up on the ascending wave the boat came. 'Now—jump!' Over she went—just in the nick of time as the minesweeper began rapidly to descend some twenty feet or more! And two brawny sailors caught her as she landed.

That was faith! First the *intellectual acceptance* of truth—she saw the rescue ship and realized its significance, and *with her mind* realized its offer of help. Then followed the *volitional* act—by an act of will she deliberately *jumped* and accepted the rescue. The jump meant a complete break with the larger ship—a leap—first into space, then to safety.

There you see faith. That is how it is with God's grace. It is offered free! The grace of pardon, the grace of power —but it must be accepted by an act of faith: by an intellectual acceptance—and a *venture on the truth*.

Grace gives, faith receives!

. . . . .

This then is the way of salvation—'by grace are ye saved through faith'. There is no doubt of our need—and what we need is offered by God as His free undeserved gift.

Have you accepted that wondrous gift? So many of us live in fear, in sin, in failure, in futility, in monotony, in bondage, in gloom, when we could be living in hope and joy and strength, in the power of the Resurrection! And yet, we still grovel when we could climb.

Is not the truth here, that we fear the cost—particularly the cost to pride? The Rev. W. M. F. Scott, who is the Chaplain of Wycliffe Hall, Oxford, has told how a man whom he was trying to help once said to him, 'Do you expect me to come before God with empty hands and outstretched arms, and tell Him my life's a failure, and that I can't live without Him? I'm damned if I will. I'm too damned proud.' He was honest, but Mr. Scott says, it was only when he got to that position that he was able to find Christ.

That's where we must get—before Christ can get us, on our knees, in utter humility, with no self-trust, no pride, no self-assurance, empty-handed, broken-hearted, dependent.

> Nothing in my hands I bring,
> Simply to Thy Cross I cling.

Sir James Young Simpson, the discoverer of chloroform, was once asked what was the greatest discovery he had ever made, and he replied: 'The greatest discovery I have ever made is that Jesus is my Saviour.'

That is the supreme discovery.

METHODIST CERTAINTY—ASSURANCE

The spirit itself beareth witness with our spirit that we are the children of God.
ROMANS viii. 16.

In the previous chapter, we discussed the primary emphasis of Methodism, which is 'salvation by faith'. In this we are to consider a doctrine which early Methodism considered as equally important, namely the doctrine of *'assurance'*.

We will approach the subject by way of a personal reminiscence—which is a parable.

I spent my boyhood in a coast town, where, when the tide recedes, there are exposed great stretches of rock which are honeycombed with thousands of clear pools teeming with all kinds of marine life—anemones, limpets, lobsters, crabs, and the like. One day my sister and I had been playing in one of these pools for some considerable time when we heard a man's raucous voice bellowing from the shore. We turned from our play, and to our utter astonishment discovered that we were entirely surrounded by water! All unnoticed, the incoming tide had crept around us so that we were completely enisled, with an expanse of perhaps thirty feet of water between us and the land. Into this water the shouter came striding, wading waist deep, to our rescue, and eventually carried both of us safely to land.

That man *saved our lives*! There was no possible doubt about it—he saved us, and we *knew it*: we were sure.

Can we be equally sure of the Saviourhood of Christ? Can we *know* that we are saved? And, if so, *how* can we know?

We Methodists claim that we *can*. One of our central

doctrines is the doctrine of *assurance*. We claim that it comes in two ways: (1) By an *inward conviction*, (2) By an *outward manifestation*—by inner certainty, and outward conduct.

We will consider each in turn.

(1) INWARD CONVICTION

Every Methodist knows the story of how John Wesley was suddenly changed from a sincere but ineffective clergyman into the most amazing revivalist the country has ever known. It's the story of a long earnest *search*, which culminated in a sudden and wonderful experience of inner illumination. Writing of it himself, Wesley said: '*An assurance* was given me that He had taken away my sins, even mine, and saved me . . .'[1]

Note the phraseology: AN ASSURANCE! Before that Wesley had THOUGHT himself saved. When asked by a Moravian pastor if he had 'the witness' in himself that Christ was his Saviour, he had fenced with the pertinent query by saying he 'hoped' Christ had died to save him. But after this Wesley was sure; and from that time on the doctrine of assurance began to permeate his sermons.

Wesley did not invent the doctrine; he simply rescued it from the theological rubbish-heap of his day. St. Paul had suggested it in his Epistles, especially in the famous Romans viii, where he says: 'the Spirit *beareth witness* with our spirit that we are sons of God.'[2]

Wesley was, as most readers will know, in the habit of always consulting his mother on matters of both thought and policy. And when in conversation with her he told her of his own assurance of salvation, she told him that although she had scarce heard of such a thing before, and certainly had never dared ask it for herself, yet a few weeks before had, while receiving the Sacrament, experienced

---

[1] *Journal of John Wesley*, vol. I, p. 476.   [2] Romans viii. 16.

such an assurance herself. This strengthened Wesley's conviction, and later in one of his writings said: 'I never yet knew one soul saved without what you call the faith of assurance.' The doctrine became one of the central emphases of Methodism.

Were there time, one could pluck numerous illustrative examples from early Methodist biography. We must be content however with one. We take the case of Peter Jaco, one of Wesley's preachers. Peter was born of serious parents, but in youth became headstrong and a great seeker of pleasure. In spite of all his frantic search for happiness, however, he was desperately miserable. Then came the Methodist preachers, and Jaco, under a conviction of sin, joined the Methodist Society. For four months those good people tried their utmost to help him— but in vain. His misery grew almost to despair. Then, suddenly one Sunday evening, while walking alone, the illumination came to him. Here is his own account: 'In that moment it seemed to me as though a new creation had taken place. I felt no guilt, no distress of any kind. My soul was filled with light and love. *I could no more doubt of my acceptance with God through Christ, than I could of my own existence*.'[1]

So it was with all Wesley's preachers. They were no icy negatives they proclaimed, but glowing *certainties*. They had assurance!

(2) OUTWARD MANIFESTATION

This is complementary to the inner conviction; it is inseparably linked with it. It *confirms* it! There is a danger of the inner conviction being self-deception. Delusions are both possible and dangerous. One man may consider himself a musical genius. He may have an overwhelming conviction on the matter! But, if everyone else holds a

[1] *Wesley's Veterans*, vol. II, p. 10, and *Early Methodist Preachers*, vol. I, p. 262.

contrary view, his own conviction must be dismissed as delusion—and therefore worthless. Our personal convictions about ourselves must have the confirmation of other people's convictions about us.

Thus, the *outward* visible evidence of salvation is REFORMATION. Outward reformation confirms the inner conviction. We accept Wesley's doctrine of assurance, not so much because of what Wesley said, but because of what he said, *plus* what he subsequently became and did! His own inner conviction had the confirmation of his outer conduct.

Consider another parable. We recall our first visit to Scotland. We approached it by car along the East Coast road, travelling from London, through Newcastle, over the Cheviots, on to Edinburgh. As the car purred its way north, we were full of eager expectation, for we had read much, and heard more, about that lovely land of rock and brogue. Presently we came to a bleak mountain place where there was a white line painted across the road, and by the wayside a great notice board proclaiming the fact that this side of the line was England, that side was Scotland! So over the line we crossed. At first we could see little difference, but we *knew* we were in Scotland because we had crossed the line and the notice board announced that all this side was Scottish territory. *We accepted, in faith, that claim.* Then, as we proceeded on our way, our inner conviction was *confirmed by outward evidence.* There was for example, the evidence of language! In the London we had left they would say, 'There ain't no daht abaht it', but here they said, 'Nae doot aboot it'! Then there was the evidence of custom—the kilts, the tam-o'-shanters, the plaids, the bagpipes. . . . Even the meals were different! (I never risked a haggis: Englanders had told me they were boiled bagpipes, and I didn't care to risk it!) And then there was the evidence of what I'll call atmosphere. Edinburgh, the wonder city with its castle on the rock, its indescribable war memorial, its St. Giles' redolent with memories of Knox, Holyrood with its memories of Mary Queen of Scots. Everywhere in that bonny North the land reeks of Scotland: heather, broom, foxgloves, poetry, history—it's a wonderful country! We can well understand the Scotsman's pride in it.

It is not unlike that with salvation. Think of it as a land —a land of promise. You approach it with eager expectation—for you have read much, and heard more, about it. Then you come to the border. There is the plain declaration: 'This side lies the land of Salvation'—but the dividing line *must be crossed!* So over you go! And once across you have the *mental certainty* that you are there! Then, as you proceed, the farther you go, the more convinced you become that you are in that glorious country! The language is different—and *you begin to speak the new language.* They used to talk about Christians speaking 'the language of Canaan'. It was a picturesque and Biblical way of describing a reality. There *is* a language of the new land, and if you are really there, you'll want to speak it. You needn't ape pious phrases—it's more a matter of accent than anything—but your friends will soon know. You remember: 'They took knowledge of them that they had been with Jesus'! It was self-evidence —like the Scotsman's accent!

We recall how soon after taking over a certain church we 'met' a men's fellowship which a predecessor had started. We were trying to 'get the feel of it' (trying to get their spiritual wavelength), and one man said: '*Oh, we don't want to talk religion. We get enough of that on Sundays!*' There was no doubt as to which side of the line that man was! He didn't *like* the language of Canaan! If he had been saved, then to speak the language would have been his greatest joy; the song of his heart would have been: 'I cannot from His praise forbear!'

Yes, there is the unmistakable evidence of language.

There is the evidence of life attitudes. When Wesley's illumination came, he said: 'I began to pray with all my might for those who had in a more especial manner despitefully used me and persecuted me.'[1]

The charitable heart is unmistakable evidence. Let your so-called Christian indulge in bitterness and slander, in caustic cynicism and harsh judgement, and you have clear evidence that his supposed salvation is spurious! St. John, who was perhaps farther advanced in the Grace of God than any other man has ever been, said: 'We know that we have passed from death to life because we love the brethren' (John iii. 14). 'Hereby know we that we are of the truth, because we love one another, not in word . . . but in deed' (verse 19).

Then there is the evidence of custom—the love of God's house and God's people, a desire to meet in fellowship and prayer, and fervency of prayer.

There is also the evidence of what, in reference to Scotland I called 'atmosphere'. It is true that the really 'saved' Christian carries about with him his own fragrant and unmistakable 'atmosphere'. It is an atmosphere of peace, of poise, of power, of blessedness, of holiness! A friend recently told us of how once he was in the presence of that great saint, C. F. Andrews. Andrews spoke no word, but my friend said he could *feel* his goodness.

Last, but not least, is the evidence of evangelical passion—a longing for others to share the bliss too! As I read Christian biography, covering the whole period of Christianity from the Acts up to our own day, I am amazed and challenged by the evangelical passion which is everywhere apparent. The Apostles had it! The Franciscans had it! The Puritans had it! The Methodists had it! Here are a few phrases plucked like flowers from such biographies: 'I yearned for souls;' 'I agonized for souls;' 'I longed to win others.' The man who has

[1] *Journal of John Wesley*, vol. I, p. 476.

been rescued from the jaws of death by the skill of a great physician *must* talk about that marvellous surgical exploit. His gratitude is both *deep* and *verbal!* So when the Great Physician has healed a sick heart! When men are really soundly saved they want both to *declare* and *share* it! The songs of their heart are:

> My heart is full of Christ, and longs
> Its glorious matter to declare!

and

> O let me commend my Saviour to you.

This, then, is the second great emphasis of Methodism—assurance! We believe that our Salvation is so unmistakable that we can *know* it—we know by inner conviction and the outer evidence of a reformed life.

As Charles Wesley puts it:

> The witness in ourselves we have,
> And all its fruits we show.

.   .   .   .   .

We end the chapter with a thumbnail sketch from real life. It sums up all we have been trying to say. It begins with comedy, moves to the brink of tragedy, and ends in victory.

About seventy years ago there was a terrible drought, and as a consequence some Primitive Methodists had met in a one-roomed cottage to pray for rain. The occupant was an elderly woman who always joined in the prayers and usually ended with the high-pitched petition, 'Lord, pour Thy blessing upon us. Let it come in bucketfuls.' A village boy named Tom Jackson believed that prayer is a co-operative concern, and decided to lend a hand. One night Tom and two pals took up positions, one by the window listening, one with a bucket of water, and Tom astride the roof by the chimney. Loud and earnest were the voices within. Presently the boy by the window whispered, 'She's started', and the second handed Tom the pail, and as the poor woman shouted, 'Send it down in bucketfuls', Tom obliged by pouring the water down the chimney! ! !

Soon tricks of this kind landed Tom in serious trouble, and one night he was obliged to flee the village to escape justice: his pranks had led him to the edge of tragedy. He fled to Sheffield, and there one night was troubled by a sermon he heard in a Methodist chapel. All night he suffered torment, but when dawn broke a decision was reached.

That night he made his way to a chapel vestry where he knew a Class Meeting would be held. An old man was arranging seats. 'What hast tha' come for, lad?'

'I've come to be converted,' Tom replied.

'Then,' said the old man, 'tha' canst soon settle that. Kneel thee down.'

The old man prayed. Then he said, 'Dost believe He will save Thee?'

'Yes.'

'Dost believe He can save thee *now*?'

'Yes.'

'Glory be to God. Thou'rt converted, lad.'

The truth is that Tom was already converted. That had happened in the morning struggle and subsequent decision; this simply ratified it. But in his heart Tom *knew*: he had *assurance*. There was the inner conviction. Now follows the outward manifestation.

You can't be saved and do nothing about it, and so Tom began to *do*. First he began teaching in Sunday school, but as he taught he became appalled at his own ignorance, so he began a course of self-education. He was an iron-worker, and in the dinner hour he preached to his work-mates. Then he began preaching in earnest, and with such power that he was offered a post as district missionary at £1 a week. He was married now and earning good money, with every prospect of advancement, but he accepted the post. Soon he was living in a vermin-infested hovel in a London slum seeking in Christ's name to win the denizens of the East End for Christ. In the power of Christ, he succeeded in taking the debris of slumdom and making of it exemplary citizens. Drunkards, gamblers, jailbirds, thieves were reformed. Along with evangelism he linked philanthropy. In the famine of 1888 he began the free feeding of hundreds of starving children, selling his own possessions to start the work. He instituted a cheap medical and legal service. He started a home for orphan lads, and homes of rest at the seaside, and so on, and always as the work grew managed to raise the necessary money for his multitudinous humanitarian enterprises. So he laboured for over sixty years.[1]

Was he saved? There is no doubt about the answer. God took the vigour and enterprise of the miscreant and directed it into redemptive channels, and *his life* proclaimed his salvation. He had his own inner assurance, but it was confirmed by these outer manifestations.

Reader, may I in all gentleness and courtesy ask you these pointed, but all-important, personal questions: Are you saved? Is your religion real? Does it carry you—or are you trying to carry it? Is it just formal and cold, or is it inward and glowing? Is it transforming, enabling, redeeming power in your life? Have you the inner assurance in your own heart, and are there the unmistakable outward manifestations in your life?

If the answer is negative, I beg you, in Christ's name, go to your knees, settle this matter with God. If you are not saved, you are missing the most wonderful and the most precious of all experiences—the one thing that makes life worth while!

Jesus not only offers us His glorious example to copy: He offers Himself, His risen self, His power, to transform us, redeem us, refresh us, use us. He comes to us as

[1] W. Potter, *Thomas Jackson of Whitechapel.*

Saviour. This, my friend, is the *Gospel*—good news. 'Live kindly and help one another' is no gospel. It is mere sentimentality. Here is the Gospel: the power of God unto salvation. You *can* be saved. You can *know* you are saved, and if you are really saved, *others will know too*.

CHAPTER III

METHODIST TEACHING ON HOLINESS

By salvation he [the Methodist] means holiness of heart and life. . . . He sees it as the life of God in the soul.

JOHN WESLEY.

THE doctrine of personal holiness is an integral and all-important part of the Methodist emphases. Wesley's declared aim was to '*spread scriptural holiness throughout the land*'.

.   .   .   .   .

What do we Methodists mean by 'scriptural holiness'? In a word we mean spiritual HEALTHINESS. The word 'holy' is a development of an Old English word, *hálig*, which literally means *whole*. To be 'holy' simply means to be spiritually healthy. When Wesley and his followers used the word, they meant nothing more or less than a soul flooded, drenched, permeated by divine life.

This holiness was beautiful. The Bible talks of the 'beauty' of holiness—and the early Methodists had that! Their little groups of converts were like clusters of chaste, lovely snowdrops growing on a foul rubbish-heap. They were clusters of moral and spiritual chastity flourishing amid amazing and widespread corruption.

England at that time was morally rotten. The Court was corrupt, and Church and peoples followed its example. Southey claimed that there never was less religion, and one of the bishops of the day said there was a torrent of iniquity.

The fires of an earlier and vigorous Nonconformity had died down into a mere dull smoulder. The Church of England was lethargic and many of its clergy actually immoral. Bear-baiting and cock-fights were popular pastimes. Some idea of the low moral tone of the day can be gathered from the fact that (in 1736) every sixth house in London was a grog shop. Gin-drinking was so heavy that there was widespread disease as the result of it. In twenty-eight years the sale of spirits had increased by seven million gallons. Grog shops openly advertised to make a man drunk for a 1d. and dead drunk for 2d., 'with straw to lie on until you recovered'. Each shop actually kept a cellar with straw, on to which to throw its helpless victims until they recovered. There were actually clubs for debauchery, and the members committed the most awful crimes on the London streets. Neither men nor women were safe. Robbery was rife, and the watchmen and constables unable to do anything about it. (These were the good old days!)

In the midst of all this there grew and flourished like chaste flowers those little centres of brave people whose highest aim was to be 'holy' according to Scriptural standards.

Their holiness was just sheer Christian goodness—Christ-likeness! There was nothing anaemic or weak about it. It was strong, robust, virile. And here the analogy of the snowdrop breaks down, for the early Methodist holiness had steel in it. It was a holiness that made for enormous sacrifices, marvellous endurance, and wondrous courage. Persecution was the frequent lot of these people, but they bore it with quietude and charity. Brutality was directed at both men and women, and their property wilfully destroyed, and yet they bore it with patience. They had in them exactly the same qualities as the early Apostles—their heroic lives made a thrilling addition to the Acts. They took insults without resentment, they accepted blows without retaliation, they were cursed, and blessed in return. This holiness of theirs expressed itself in multitudinous benevolent and social activities; it claimed that to love God with all the heart means also to love one's neighbour as oneself.

We offer here two thumbnail sketches of early Methodist characters as actual examples of this virile goodness.

The first is John Fletcher of Madeley. He had been born in Switzerland, and as a youth had become a soldier of fortune. A series of accidents brought him to England, where he joined the Methodists and became a vicar. His parish was full of rough colliers and iron-workers. It is literally true to say they were wild and half civilized, but Fletcher loved and served them with a wondrous devotion. He was utterly brave and regardless of danger. He was utterly unselfish and devoted all his rents to charitable purposes, and even sold his own furniture and clothes in order to help others. He would be astir and at work at 5 a.m. and not return home till two the next morn. This sacrificial faithfulness and invincible benevolence eventually won love in response, and his church, which at first was empty, began to overflow.

Fletcher was a scholar of considerable attainment, and when the Predestinarians began their caustic and bitter attacks on Methodism, he took up his pen in Methodism's defence. 'But', writes his biographer, 'if ever true Christian charity was manifested in polemical writing, it was by Fletcher of Madeley.'

So he lived, a life of moral and spiritual robust health, a holy life, and when he died Wesley wrote: 'I have known many excellent men, holy in heart and life, but one equal to him I have not known, one so uniformly and deeply devoted to God.'

But Fletcher, of course, was an exceptional man. He was like the brilliant star which in the dawn light outshines all the others. I have chosen him because he was one of the leaders of early Methodism. Wesley had chosen Fletcher to succeed him, but Fletcher died first.

Now consider a common ranker—and a woman. I take the case of Grace Murray. When she first met the Methodists, she was a gay young wife of a sea captain. Their marriage was tremendously happy. But soon sorrow crushed the music from her young heart. Her little child died, and Grace was broken-hearted. Grief changed her spontaneous gaiety to distraught anguish. It was just then that John Wesley rode into London, and Grace heard him preach. Never had she heard anything like it before. The calm little man, with all his frame tense with sincerity and conviction, was proclaiming a God, not of terror, but of love, and Grace found a new life in Christ.

And now the drama begins. Her husband returned from sea to find a new wife; she was changed, and he didn't like the new Grace; she was too good for the pleasure-loving sailor. So, instead of offering her love, as he had always done before, he tried to scorch and burn the goodness out of her with the fire of his anger. If she would not leave the Methodists, he said, he would put her in a madhouse! 'You shall leave them or me,' he stormed. And the new-born Grace gave the reply: 'I love you above anyone else on earth, *but I will leave you and all that I have sooner than I will leave Christ.*'

Then yelled the enraged husband, 'I will go as far as ships can sail'.

Calmly Grace replied: 'I could lay down my life for you but I cannot destroy my soul.'

So to sea he went again—and never returned.[1]

Do you get a glimpse of Scriptural holiness there? A holiness with courage in it. A love of God so deep and strong that all other loves dwindle before it? A gratitude to Christ so overwhelming that it results in a loyalty as firm and impregnable as Gibraltar's rock!

*   *   *   *   *

So far we have considered what early Methodist holiness was. Now we will consider what it DID.

It cleansed the life of Britain. It brought strength and

[1] G. Elsie Harrison, *Methodist Good Companions*, p. 19.

stability back into English character, and it set in motion moral and spiritual forces which reached right across the world, and right through the ages—up to our own day.

Let me present the truth in a parable. Imagine a well. At the base of it there is a spring of clear, ice-cold, life-giving water. Unfortunately, however, the well is clogged with dirt and debris, and so always the water is contaminated and rendered useless for human use and refreshment. Then comes a man who cleans the well! The dirt and debris are removed, and into the cleaned well the pellucid spring waters rise. Now thirsty men come to drink, and for miles around, men and beasts are refreshed by the life-giving water.

There is a parable of what Wesley did by spreading 'Scriptural holiness throughout the land'.

The well represents the Church. For many years the clear waters of Puritanism had been striving to rise within the well. But the Church was clogged with dirt and debris. As we have seen, even the clergy were corrupt, indifferent, and often immoral.

Then came Wesley and the Methodists, with their teaching and holiness. It was like a cleansing process, and into the clean well the pure waters rose, giving life, refreshment, and health to all who would drink. Everything was enriched—the Church, national morals, and politics.

Take, first, the Church. We must remember that at first Methodism was a movement *within* the Church, but even when the Church as a whole drove Wesley and his followers out, there were many men still in the Church who were enriched and enthused by Methodism. William Romaine was one. He was Vicar of the famous St. George's, Hanover Square. He caught Methodism's spirit, and as a result his success as a preacher became a positive embarrassment to his regular worshippers, for they could not get seats in their own church! His emphases were virtually Methodism's emphases: salvation by faith and holiness of life. When he first began this new preaching there were only six or seven Evangelical clergy in all England, but when he died there were more than five hundred!

Then the morals of England began to change. Methodist holiness became as a transforming power within the country: it was like 'salt', it purified.

The story of the political repercussions of Methodist holiness is a long and amazing one. Suffice to say here that historians of repute agree that it was Methodism which saved Britain from the French Revolution, and that it was the life-giving stream of Methodist holiness, flowing from Wesley, which finally led to the abolition of slavery and of child labour and the flogging of women, to prison reform, protection of animals, prohibition of spring-guns, improved sanitation, the rise of the Sunday schools, orphanages, the formation of the Religious Tract Society, the Church Missionary Society, and the British and Foreign Bible Society.

Now, the point of all this lies just here. Does not the world to-day need a new Wesley? Does not the world need these three distinctive Methodist emphases more than anything else: salvation by faith, assurance, holiness? Religion in Britain and the Continent is at an appallingly low ebb! Indifference is everywhere. The indifference is a breeding ground for future cynicism and immorality: for without vital religion a nation is like a ship without a rudder. Germany is a glaring example.

Europe to-day needs nothing so much as a spread of Scriptural holiness such as the early Methodists taught and lived.

.   .   .   .   .

What was the secret of this holiness?

Those men and women had a *divine power operative within them*. There was active within them an inner energy—a mighty, moving power; a power that put nerve and vigour into the spent will; a power which conquered the terrific onslaught of passion; a power that was an incentive to go 'conquering and to conquer'.

It is important, I think, to emphasize this. These men and women were not holy by *self-effort*. They were in the grip of a power other than themselves. It was not a case of what they did for God; rather it was what God did for them—of what God did *for* them, and *in* them, and *through* them.

Their new-born souls were indeed 'temples of the Holy Spirit'. They were incarnations of the divine spirit. It was *God in* them. They drew supplies from omnipotence.

As the length of my ministry has increased, I have realized more and more how important it is to grasp, and live by, this truth.

Only God can save a soul! Only God can make one holy! As I review my own Christian life and my ministry, I become poignantly conscious of this: that the times of my failure have always been the times of my *self-effort*: and the times of my success the times when I have relied on God—when I have worked not for God, but as an instrument in the hands of God, actuated, empowered, generated by His Spirit. In other words, the times of self-surrender.

God calls us to holiness. That is our *privilege*. Britain and the world needs holiness: that is our duty, but we cannot be holy of ourselves. We have to come to God, in penitence, humility, expectancy, submission—and putting ourselves completely into His hands. ' Move at the impulse of His will.'

Our supreme need is to pray for the endowment of *power*. I often reflect on the significance of that exhortation of Jesus to 'wait for the Pentecostal power'.

The men to whom He spake knew Him; they loved Him. They knew the risen Jesus, the truth of their resources had dawned in their minds; but something was still necessary—and the risen Lord told them to wait and pray for the promise of the Father. And it was that—Pentecostal power—that made them into conquering Apostles.

We know Jesus; we love Him. We are aware of our resources in Him! But are we powerful? Are we glowing? Are we conquering? Perhaps we too need to wait and pray until we be endowed with power from on high.

I urge you to this—pray. Pray until the Holy Spirit throbs in your heart and speaks in your speech; pray till you become triumphant and joyous.

CHAPTER IV

METHODISM'S STRESS UPON UNIVERSAL GRACE

Grace for every soul is free,
All may hear the effectual call;
All the light of life may see,
All may feel He died for all.

Away on the horizon can be seen colliery shaftheads and buildings silhouetted against a sky which is as blue as a hedge-sparrow's egg. In the foreground is a stretch of open country bathed in June loveliness. Right in the centre of the picture is an enormous crowd, probably 3,000 strong! On the crowd's fringe are drawn up a few private carriages, and their owners are using the high driving seats as vantage points from which to survey the vast concourse. The crowd consists chiefly of ordinary people, many of them unspeakably poor, for it is just the beginning of the machine age, when the new discoveries of coal and iron, and the invention of the steam engine, have suddenly placed unexpected means of wealth into men's eager grasp. Indeed, opportunities for the exploitation of human life and labour are wellnigh unrestrained. Many of the men are miners, with faces as black as the coal which they excavate. Most of the women are poorly clad, with dishevelled hair, wrinkled skins, and decayed teeth. Only a few of them are pretty. There are also blacksmiths, joiners, farm-labourers, and the like—a motley throng! In the midst of this multitude there stands a clergyman holding the throng spell-bound with his oratory. He is John Wesley.

He is small of stature, cultured in speech, and quiet in manner. He is forty years of age, and stands raised above the crowd on a slight eminence. For fifteen years he has lived and worked in the cultured circles of Oxford University, first as student, then as Don. After that he resided in the new colony of Georgia, attempting to convert the Indian natives! His efforts, however, have ended in terrible failure. Then, back in England again, there had come to him that amazing spiritual experience which has warmed his heart and changed his life. And so he stands here amid the vast crowd, holds out those aristocratic hands, and cries:

> Sent by my Lord, on you I call,
>   The invitation is to all,
> Come, all the world; come, sinner, thou,
>   All things in Christ are ready now.
>
> My message as from God receive,
>   Ye all may come to Christ, and live:
> O let His love your hearts constrain,
>   Nor suffer Him to die in vain.

That was how John Wesley preached! Indeed, that was how all those early Methodists preached! They proclaimed a Grace that was *Universal*—it was for *all*. They believed that all men needed saving, *all* men could be saved, *all* could know themselves saved, and *all* be saved to the uttermost.

To us, of course, there does not appear to be anything unusual or startling about such claims. To us they are commonplace emphases. But they were not commonplace to Wesley's generation. In those days they were startling and breath-taking.

Roughly speaking, there were three attitudes to religion in Wesley's day. (1) Among the poor and illiterate there was widespread indifference. The masses were literally heathen, neither thinking about nor caring for the things of God. (2) In more informed circles there was a scornful 'free-thought', which styled itself 'Deism'. It claimed that God was like an *absentee* Landlord. It openly and caustically scoffed at all forms of religion. (3) In religious circles there was Calvinism—particularly that form of Calvinism which stresses 'predestination'. Throughout the Church it was generally believed that some men were chosen by God to be saved; others were destined to be damned. The chosen were the 'elect'—to use one of their own phrases, they were kings 'incog.', travelling disguised like pilgrims to his dominions above! Others, however, were not so fortunate. Theirs was a grim fate—inescapable damnation! 'One in twenty', said one of the preachers of the day, is 'elected'; nineteen in twenty are reprobate. The elect shall be saved, do what they will; the reprobate shall be damned, do what they can.'

The Wesleys refused to accept such a theory; to them it was both unscriptural and unreasonable—indeed, monstrous! So they set out to oppose it in every way that was open to them—in sermons, in pamphlets, in hymns. And they smashed it! It was the Wesleys who dealt the death-blow to Calvinism in England.

Their attitude was well and lyrically expressed in one of Charles's poems:

> And shall I, Lord, confine Thy love,
>   As not to others free?
> And may not *every* sinner prove
>   The grace that found out *me?*
>
> Doom them an endless death to die,
>   From which they could not flee:—
> No, Lord! Thine inmost bowels cry
>   Against that dire decree!

There is no doubt that the whole world is deeply indebted to Calvin. There was about his theology something great and tremendous: in breadth of conception it stands unrivalled. Moreover, it produced strong character and great men. Calvin's social teaching led to great reforms, and countries like Scotland benefited tremendously.

Calvinism was undoubtedly one of the great creative forces of history. Indeed, one cannot help but feel that our own generation would do well to recapture Calvin's emphasis on the supremacy of God.

These were not the things that the Wesleys controverted. Their chief objection was to the doctrine of predestination. This they could not accept. It was unscriptural! In their Gospels, they read of a Jesus who cried invitingly: 'Come unto me, *all*.' They found it impossible to visualize that gracious Personality condemning men wholesale to damnation. In the Gospel of St. John they read how Christ's most intimate friend reported Him as saying: 'God so loved the world, that He gave His only begotten Son, that *whosoever* believeth on Him should *not perish* but have everlasting life' (John iii. 16). These universalities they found echoed in the Epistles: in the Epistle to the Romans they read that Christ was 'delivered up for us *all*' (Romans viii. 32). 'The Lord is not willing that any should perish, but that *all* should come to repentance' is what they read in the Second Epistle of St. Peter's (2 Peter iii. 9). In the Epistle to Timothy, they read: 'He gave Himself a ransom for *all*' (1 Timothy ii. 6).

So, as their theology developed, there was about it a universal sweep. And nowhere was that universality more convincingly expressed than in Charles Wesley's hymns. Charles's hymns were John's theology set to music, and all of them abound in universal invitations:

> O that the world might taste and see
>   The riches of His grace!
> The arms of love that compass me
>   Would *all* mankind embrace.

This, then, is the fourth great emphasis of Methodism: the universality of God's Grace!

.   .   .   .   .

It is well to note, we think, that there are two sides to this teaching, as there are two sides to a penny! The other side of universality is *individuality*. Christ died for *all*. That is true, but that *all* includes *me*—and *you!* So through our history, we Methodists have stressed this individuality. When Wesley's heart was 'warmed', the Cross became personalized; he cried: 'He loved *me*, and gave Himself for *me*'.

Has the Cross been personalized for you? Have you ever reached a point in life when you could say with Wesley: 'He loved *me*'?

This Grace of God which is universally offered, has to be individually accepted.

Consider an imaginative picture. A deep blue sky, and from its depths a pitiless sun beating down on a great swaying crowd. Everywhere there are the gay colours of the East, and everywhere the dirt and flies of the East too. The crowd seems to be excited and there is prevalent the same sort of atmosphere as one finds at an English boxing bout or cup final.

We push our way in among the folk and inquire of an olive-skinned Jew what all the 'to-do' is about. Looking at us through cunning little eyes, he surprisingly asks: 'Don't you know? Haven't you heard?'

'No,' we explain. 'We are only newly arrived in Jerusalem. What's all this excitement?'

'A crucifixion,' the man casually volunteers and he spits in the dust.

'A crucifixion! That's Roman justice, isn't it? What's been afoot? Anarchy?'

'No,' the man sneers. 'Nothing much—a couple of robbers and a rebel.'

Just then the crowd sways as a wave of excitement sweeps across it like a summer breeze across a field of waving corn, and at that moment a cross is raised aloft, sways about and jolts into its socket on a hill summit. Then another, and then a third.

To our English eyes, the whole scene is revolting in the

extreme, and we wonder how men and women can look on at such cruelty unmoved.

But, it is the central Figure wins our sympathy. Limply, He hangs suspended by those pierced hands. On his brow He wears a crown of thorns. The little spurts of blood flow freely down His anguished cheeks. In His eyes great tears glisten like jewels. The spittle of a Roman legionary is congealed on His beard. And as we look, a voice seems to speak—more to our hearts than our ears—saying: 'He died there for you.'

Has that stupendous truth ever yet stormed the citadel of your soul? Has it come to you, as it did to Wesley, as it has to millions of others, like the spear that pierced Christ's heart? Have you ever *seen* it, and realized it—and accepted it. Have you ever seen it with clear, inner perception, so that in an agony of apprehension you have cried: 'Love so amazing, so divine!'

That is my consuming purpose now, to help you to see it, to realize, as never before.

> See Him set forth before your eyes,
>   That precious, bleeding sacrifice!
> His offered benefits embrace,
>   And freely now be saved by grace.

So far we have not even adumbrated any theory of the Atonement, and it may help the reader if, before proceeding farther, we endeavour to do so.

The author has read numerous books on this great theme, each expressing a different view. None, however, has completely satisfied his mind. Perhaps every theory contains some element of truth, but none of them the whole truth. There can be no doubt that by His death Jesus did something for mankind that no one else has ever done. It appears true, too, that He did something on the Cross which could not have been done in any other way. What was that something?

He effected a reconciliation. Paul said: 'God was in Christ reconciling the world unto Himself' (2 Corinthians v. 19). Thus the awkward word 'atonement', which literally means at-one-ment. Man has somehow or other become estranged from God. Ancient theology said that he 'fell' from grace. The Bible figured it pictorially in that incomparable story of the Garden of Eden, where Adam, by eating the forbidden fruit, brought upon himself a tragic banishment.

There have been those who claimed that God was angry with man for his sin, and needed His wrath appeasing, and Jesus, they affirm, died in order to pacify the enraged deity. Others have asserted that divine Justice had to be satisfied, and so Jesus died so that man could be liberated from the demands of that Justice.

There is no doubt that these theories helped other generations. But they do not help us. Their weakness, so it appears to us, lies in their failure to understand Christ's teaching about the nature of God. The God of these theories was an Eastern despot, angry and revengeful, but even a cursory reading of the Gospels is enough to convince one that our Lord held no such ideas. To Him God was no sheik! He was a father. He was merciful. He was LOVE.

One of the most unique things about the teaching of Jesus was the suggestion that God was a SEEKING God. As Rudolf Otto, one of the most eminent modern scholars, has said: 'The real Christian God, whom neither theism nor any other religion whatsoever conceives in the same way, is a seeking God, i.e. the God who seeks the lost.'[1]

Does not this bring us right to the heart of the truth? Is not the truth just this: that God, being love, has created mankind for Himself, and His desire (above everything else) is a loving response from His own children. Ever He is seeking such a response. But man persists in being deaf to the appeals.

[1] *The Kingdom of God and the Son of Man*, pp. 393-4.

And so the Divine Parent has sent His messengers to men in the patriarchs, the prophets, the preachers, but their appeals have passed misunderstood or unheeded. Jesus came as the final messenger—God's final appeal. But the final appeal even was rejected. Men were so blind in their selfishness that they could not see! And so, other things having failed, Jesus in His love went to the UTTERMOST LIMIT, He accepted the Cross as the final attempt to achieve His purpose of bringing men to God.

The Cross was God in Jesus saying: 'This is how I love!' The arms of Jesus cruelly outstretched on the wood of the Roman gibbet were outstretched on God's behalf, saying, as He had so often done before: 'COME. . . . Come to God's heart of love. . . .' And as men since that day have heard the story of the suffering Christ, they have suddenly realized this truth, and they have come to God, reconciled! Atoned!

The Cross stuns and awakens men to the realization of the truth as nothing else does. When a missionary had told the story of the death of Jesus to some natives, one of them cried: 'O Jesus, away from there! Away from there! That is not your place; it is mine.' That is how most of us feel when we really see and understand the Cross.

So God's appeal comes to our hearts to-day, as it has been doing to the hearts of men ever since that first Good Friday, . . . and the message is still the same: 'COME'. Be reconciled to God.

Do you remember Dinah Morris in George Eliot's beautiful novel, *Adam Bede?* Dinah was a Methodist girl preacher (George Eliot drew her from an actual character who lived at Wirksworth). And there is a moving scene where Dinah preaches on the village green. For a whole hour she holds her rustic audience spellbound as she proclaims the unsearchable riches of Christ. And then she ends her sermon with these words:

Dear friends, come and take this blessedness; it is

offered to you: it is the good news that Jesus came to preach to the poor. It is not like the riches of this world, so that the more one gets the less the rest can have. God is without end; His love is without end:

> Its streams the whole creation reach,
>   So plenteous is the store,
> Enough for *all*, enough for each,
>   Enough for evermore.

So I appeal to you.

Do not pass the Cross unheeding. I beseech you, don't be one of the vast masses who are merely indifferent. Salvation is offered to all—to you. The choice is *yours*.

> When Jesus came to Golgotha,
>   They hanged Him on a tree;
> They drave great nails thro' hands and feet,
>   And made a Calvary;
> They crowned Him with a crown of thorns,
>   Red were His wounds and deep,
> For those were crude and cruel days,
>   And human life was cheap.
>
> When Jesus came to . . .
>   They simply passed Him by,
> They never hurt a hair of Him,
>   They simply let Him die;
> For men had grown more tender,
>   And they would not give Him pain.
> They only just passed down the street,
>   And left Him in the rain.
>
> Still Jesus cried, 'Forgive them,
>   For they know not what they do';
> And still it rained the winter rain
>   That drenched Him thro' and thro'.
> The crowds went home, and left the streets
>   Without a soul to see,
> But Jesus crouched against the wall
>   And cried for Calvary.[1]

[1] G. A. Studdert Kennedy, *The Unutterable Beauty*, p. 24.

That is the kind of refusal, I fear, that many are extending towards Jesus to-day. Nothing very militant, nothing brutally unkind, but refusals for all that.

Refusals can be very polite, but what irony there is in our modern polite refusals! They are courteous—but grim!

CHAPTER V

METHODISTS' BELIEF IN DIVINE JUDGEMENT

In my opinion, the greatest need of to-day is some teaching of judgement, or the spiritual equivalent of hell.

J. ERNEST RATTENBURY, D.D.

IF you had wished to join the 'Methodists' in the days of John Wesley, you would have been asked this startling question: 'Do you desire to *flee from the wrath to come?*' And 'the wrath to come' would have been to you a very real and terrible possibility! Do we still believe this sort of thing, or can we dismiss it as a crudity out of which we have long since grown?

We no longer, of course, hold the idea that hell is a material place in the Hereafter, where men suffer eternal tortures in a lake of fire. Not only has modern science compelled us to dismiss such an idea, but we are learning at last that the Bible was written by Easterners to whom our Western literalism was unknown. Not only so, but such an idea seems to be incompatible with the conception of God as love.

But because we have discarded the literalism of former generations, let us not make the mistake of supposing we have also dismissed the spiritual and moral truths those material metaphors stood for. That material *Hell* stood for God's Judgement. We no longer believe in a fiery-furnace hell, but we still believe in Divine Judgement. That we cannot escape. All life as we know it is shot through with judgement.

Turn, first, to the Bible. Early in this lovely book you have that beautiful old story of the Garden of Eden. The story stresses three salient truths: (1) That there is given to every man the power of free choice—free will. (2) Each person is at liberty to choose between one of two ways— good and bad. (3) The choice of bad always brings with it terrible results—punishment.

Now these three truths are echoed all the way through the Bible. In the story of the Israelites' wilderness wanderings you see them graphically illustrated. Over and over again the Israelites choose the wrong, and always suffering follows.

In the Prophets you have the same thing. Every one of those noble men thundered a warning against wrongdoing; those warnings are some of the most terrible utterances in all literature. And always the warning proved right. Wrong-doing inevitably and inexorably brought its own grim reward. At times the punishments were delayed, but always ultimately they came.

The truth is that the Bible in one way is the most terrible book in the world. It is a strange mixture of tenderness and terribleness. It woos and it warns! It offers redemption, but it also warns of retribution. The New Testament is just as terrible as the Old.

It is true that Jesus was sublimely tender, but he was also startlingly terrible. The same lips that said to some, 'Come unto me', also thundered, 'Depart from me'. The same man who forgave a sinful woman also fired his condemnation at religious hypocrites. The hands that caressed wee bairns also wielded a whip to redress a scandal. There are amongst the parables of Jesus some most startling sayings and warnings about the final judgements of God: it will be like a drag-net being pulled ashore, the good fish will be selected, the bad rejected: it will be like a shepherd dividing sheep from goats; it will be like wheat and tares being separated, the tares to be destroyed, the wheat kept. If you want to extract judgement from the New Testament, then it is a new Jesus you must find.

Such is the teaching of the Bible. Now we will turn to life itself. Life speaks of judgement too.

Consider, for example:

(1) The realm of mind and spirit. Here is a man. In his youth there open out before him several roads of opportunity. Here is the road of unselfish service, here is the road of commercial integrity, and here is the road of *unscrupulous* success. He chooses the latter. Deliberately he turns his back on the Light as it shines in Christ. He drugs his conscience, and not too scrupulously begins to climb the ladder of success. Gold is the means of ascent, and he bends all the power of a rich personality to getting gold. Lust for power becomes a passion. He works early and late. Friends go, culture goes, even human love—all are sacrificed to ambition.

And he succeeds. Eventually he becomes an industrial prince. He is sought for by all, but not for himself: *only for his gold.* The Church seeks him—to open bazaars! Philanthropy seeks him—for financial support. The world seeks him: society ladies want him to add one more notability to their parties. Everybody seeks him, because of what he *has.* No one seeks him for what he *is! And there is his judgement.* Let him lose his wealth and he loses everything. The judgement of a man of this sort is that he has had the opportunity to cultivate so many moral and spiritual things, and has neglected his opportunities, and now he stands self-condemned. 'What does it profit a man if he gain the whole world and lose his soul?' When the moment of death comes, it is, after all, only the soul that matters.

(2) Now step over into the realm of the body. It was God's desire that the human body should be the temple of the Holy Spirit. What a lovely phrase! A temple is a place of beauty, a place of prayer. It's a sacred place—the dwelling-place of God. But men desecrate the lovely shrine.

Here is an actual example. It is a sad story, and very delicate, but we must not be afraid of facing grim facts. (Probably, if we had faced them a bit more bravely in the past, we should not have been in our sorry plight to-day.)

Two boys went to school together. Their parents were friends. Both their mothers were saints. Each lad was shown the right ways of life with unmistakable clearness. One boy, however, deliberately chose the wrong. It is a sordid story, a disgusting one: 'kicking over the traces' and disregarding both warnings and moral laws. He had a pretty long run. Drink, gambling, and the like; the wild oats were sown with prodigality. Then came the reckoning. The bill was a long one! It began with a broken-hearted mother, included a ruined home life, and ran its length with a sorry list of human sufferings. Here is one item from the catalogue. One day that man folded a bairn in his arms, his child. It *was epileptic and blind*. And, as the man looked into those sightless eyes, he knew that it *was he who had struck out their* sight. As he held the poor wee thing, he stood condemned. In that bairn's face he saw the Christ face, and a voice within his own heart said with unmistakable clearness: 'Inasmuch as ye have done it unto the least of these, ye have done it unto me.' That was his judgement.

(3) Consider, now, the realm of collective affairs. No man can live to himself alone. God has so ordained that human life be based upon the pattern of the family. In the one family all benefit by the goodness and industry of one, and also all are liable to suffer for the slackness or badness of the one. The family assets are shared, but so too are the *family liabilities*. This is why the baby in the previous story had to suffer. We are all bound together by inescapable bonds—and our sins and virtues act and react in the other members of the family.

Thus the calamities of to-day!

To-day is a judgement day for the whole world. For so many years men have lived in self and sin, and thought not of the wrath to come. Heedlessly, the world has plunged on, pursuing its cruel, competitive commercialism, selling its soul so often for gold, neglecting children, exploiting the weak, oppressing, becoming, as many of our Victorian ancestors did, intoxicated with success and prosperity: becoming bloated with self-sufficiency, and then came the day of judgement!

It is said that 'chickens come home to roost'. It is true: and the grim truth is that they do not return as chickens; they return as eagles, hawks, and vultures. The social injustices of Victorian times brought their inevitable results in 1914. But we did not understand the meaning of it all; we were stupid and blind, and when we had a chance to put things right we just lapsed into selfishness again. The opportunities slipped by. Again the wind was sown, and now the whirlwind is being reaped.

In the roar of ten million guns, in the sobs of widows and orphans, the groans of the wounded and dying, in the awful agony of war, the chickens come home to roost! I look at this battlefield world and hear a voice say: 'This is judgement. This is what greed, self, lust, godlessness mean. They inevitably and inexorably bring their own results: this is godless commerce, godless diplomacy, godless pleasure working itself out to its logical conclusion.'

But, you may say, what is God's purpose in it all? Doesn't all this point to a cruel God? After all, no human parent would punish a child as ruthlessly as God seems to be punishing men to-day.

I have two things to say about that. First, I do not think that God has imposed this punishment in the same way as one may determine an act of cruelty. God does not say: 'Oh, these men are sinful. I'll send a war to punish them.' Rather, I think God puts us in a world that has *limits*. A material world must have limits. And the disregard of those limits will inevitably bring suffering.

I can illustrate this truth in this way.

Supposing you have a son. You love him, and because you love him you give him a bicycle. As soon as you make your loving gift, you make it possible for that lad to hurt both himself and others. To be safe, he must obey rules. He must keep his brakes in order, he must keep the machine in control, he must keep to the road and obey the rules of the road.

Now, we'll suppose that lad neglects his brakes and disregards the rules. He is going down a steep hill. He takes his hands off his handle-bars. He swerves. He tries to catch the handle-bars and jam on the brakes to regain control. The brakes won't act. He comes a cropper. A friend is following at top speed—also no proper control. He can't stop or swerve in time, and falls on top of your lad's bicycle and body. The friend is killed.

You have not inflicted punishment on either of them. You love them, but your love has led to the tragedy! Nevertheless, the accident is not *your* fault. It is due to *their* folly and disobedience. So it is with God and man. God gives to his sons the bicycles of free will. The gift is a gift of love. But man misuses the gift. He disregards the rules, and he brings *calamity on himself*—and others suffer too.

My second point is that the punishments of life are limitations imposed by God with a *benevolent purpose*.

Think of life as a great arterial road. The Great North Road is such a one. It is straight, smooth, and wide! But not too wide! If it were too wide, it would lose its value. It is its very limitedness that gives it direction. Its limits are marked by kerbstones, hedges, banks, and fences. Now, I can travel along that road in one direction and it will lead me home. If I go the other direction, I travel farther from home. In peacetime I can go by car and

E

speed gaily along, and in a wonderfully short time be in my father's home. That's the design of the road. To facilitate travel from one point to another. Its purpose is benevolent. But if I am careless or foolish, I can disregard the road's limits: I can drive on the path, I can say 'be hanged' to limits, I'm off into a hedge—and at sixty miles per hour plough into the hedge. But if I do, I hurt myself, and probably others too!

The county council who made the hedge have hurt me! But not deliberately. Their purpose was benevolent. *It is my disregard of the limits that hurts.* So with life. If we deliberately and persistently disregard the limits placed by God with benevolent intent, then we suffer: that is our judgement.

Now, God's purpose and supreme desire in making the road and putting boundaries is simply that we may travel thereon to Himself—travel home.

It was Torrey, I think, who used to tell a moving story of a prodigal daughter. She had left a good home for the allurements of Chicago. For many months nothing was heard of her, and at last, in desperation, her mother approached an evangelist in that great city. 'Can you help me to find my daughter?' the mother pleaded.

'What are you prepared to do?' he asked.

'Anything,' the mother replied.

Then followed a strange set of instructions. 'Go home', said the evangelist. 'Get your photograph taken. Get a hundred prints. Get them as large as you can, and bring them to me.'

The mother did as she was told, and arrived one day with a hundred large photographs. The evangelist then asked her to sit down and write under each photograph these words: 'COME HOME.'

'Now,' said the evangelist, 'will you give me permission to go round the city and pin these pictures in a hundred saloons in Chicago?' It was a big thing to ask, but the mother agreed, and so in a hundred dens of infamy in that notoriously wicked city the photographs appeared.

One night soon after, the lost daughter entered one of those saloons with a party of revellers. The picture pulled her eye! Her mother! She read the inscription: 'COME HOME.' The message had reached its desired destination. It broke the lassie's heart. In a very short time she was back home embraced in her mother's arms.

At the end of every road in life there stands a picture of God! That picture is Calvary's Cross, and all it says is: 'COME HOME.'

But someone may ask: What about the final judgement? Do I believe in that?

Yes. I do.

Wesley once preached a rather terrible sermon on the Great Assizes. I dare not do that. But I feel certain it must come. If it is all a myth, then a good deal of the New Testament and teaching of Jesus just simply does not make sense.

There are four things I believe about that great reckoning.

(1) We shall be revealed as we really are. All masks and shams and bluff will be of no avail.

(2) Many will be surprised at the judgement passed. Jesus often tried to impress this upon people. Many who were self-righteous would not pass God's tests; and others who thought little of themselves would be accepted by Him.

(3) Those who have had poor chances here will be judged according to *those chances*.

(4) No man can be finally lost until all the resources of omnipotence have been exhausted.

My final word is one of urgency.

Jesus once told a startling parable of a closed door. He described a typical Eastern crowd clamouring around the door of a house where a feast was to be held. Eastern etiquette, you remember, always welcomes anybody. And so round the door sways a struggling, swearing crowd, each eagerly seeking admittance, but the master of the feast orders the door to be barred. The elbowing throng is indignant. Some shout out that they are relatives. Some wave credentials, but 'NO'—the door is barred.

The point of the parable was that there was an urgency about salvation. It is not a matter for debate, but *direct action*.

EPILOGUE

IMAGINE a comfortable drawing-room with a bright fire glowing in the grate. In the easy chairs on either side of the hearth two men are lounging luxuriously. One of them is a young flight-lieutenant in the R.A.F.; the other is a man of about fifty, greyed about the temples and immaculate in dress. Slowly the airman lights a cigarette and flings the burnt match into the fire. 'Well,' he says at length, 'it'll soon be over now, Uncle; and then, back to "Civvy Street" to the grand work of reconstruction: the building of a brave new world!'

'Do you really think it will be a brave new world?' asks the uncle.

'Of course,' affirms the other with eagerness. 'For what else are we fighting?'

'I'm not so sure,' reflects the other man as he puffs a cloud of cigar smoke high into the air. 'There are two tendencies in modern life which make me very apprehensive.'

'Oh, what are they?' asks the nephew.

'One is the appalling danger of *mass-produced personality*; and the other the amazing spate of *moral laxity*.'

'Mass-produced personality!' echoes the other. 'Whatever do you mean by that?'

'I mean,' the uncle explains, 'there is a danger developing in our midst of whose grim possibilities we have not yet become aware. You and I are living in a very wonderful age, an age of astonishing inventions, wireless, aviation, and the like. Have you ever realized that some of the inventions which at present *appear* to be such blessings to us may become, not only a danger, but a terrible curse?'

'Well, I suppose that in a dim sort of way I have,' reflects the other. 'You mean that aeroplanes can be made to bomb cities and all that sort of thing?'

'No. I wasn't thinking quite on that line. I was thinking of the amazing power of "mass suggestions" which lie in the radio, the cinemas, and the Press. Were you ever in Germany in the years immediately preceding the war?'

'No. I was at school then and never had the chance to travel.'

'Well, I knew Germany fairly well. What amazed me was how completely in an astonishingly short time Hitler was able to stamp his own ideas and desires upon the *whole* nation. In a few short years, youths who were once nice, kind and gentlemanly like you became swaggering Storm Troopers, who inflicted appalling cruelty on the Jews: and fellows who had a year or two previously been bright, fair-haired laddies at school became regimented, cruel, fanatical Nazis. How did Hitler do it?'

'Propaganda, I suppose.'

'Of course! He collared the Press, the radio, the cinemas, and the schools, and the rest was easy. By continually drumming his ideas and desires into the eyes and ears of the nation through these agencies, he eventually changed a whole nation's psychology. Now do you see what I mean by mass-produced personality?'

'Yes, I do,' answers the nephew. 'But do you really think that we in England are as liable to be influenced by propaganda as was Germany?'

'I do; we are all in danger! Every day, through the Press, the radio, and the screen we are unconsciously absorbing standardized ideas—and the ultimate result will be standardized personalities. Now, when I was a lad there were scores of men in the town where I lived who had the most vivid personalities. They had little

ɔr no education—but they had *individuality*. They were
ɔriginal! Their conversation was spiced with witty and
pithy sayings, they had views of their own, and they
stuck to them! Lots of these old fellows went to the
Methodist chapels of the town. Some were local preachers.
They were great politicians in their way. They were
deeply interested in some of the great issues of the day—
Home Rule, the Education Bill, temperance reform, and
the like. There was then what was called a Noncon-
formist Conscience.'

'Yes, I've read of that.'

'Well, these old chaps—they were Nonconformists!
Nowadays the tendency is all *conformity*; and that's my
point. The whole tendency of modern mechanized life
is a terrible mechanical uniformity. We're all gradually
becoming *de*personalized! Individuality is disappearing.
You can almost prophesy what people will say and do
nowadays—what their favourite paper says to-day, they
say to-morrow!'

There is a long pause in the conversation, and the
two men smoke in silence. Then, throwing a cigarette
end into the fire, the airman says: 'I hadn't thought of
all this before.' And then: 'What was the other thing
about modern life which you said alarmed you, Uncle?'

'The spate of moral laxity,' replies the other. 'I expect
you see evidence of it in your sphere, don't you?'

'In a way, yes.'

'You seem rather reluctant to admit it. You know,
don't you, how alarming has been the spread of venereal
disease?'

'Yes, of course I do know a bit about that.'

'And you know how enormously drinking has increased
in the last few years, particularly among girls?'

'Yes.'

'You know too, I suppose, that the figures for divorce
are higher than they have ever been?'

'No. I didn't know that.'

'I'm told that in factories and offices the amount of petty pilfering which is going on is unimaginable; that people will lie glibly and cheerfully—considering the only thing of importance their own advantage or security. Gambling is becoming almost a mania.'

'I never knew before, Uncle, that you were such a moralist!' the nephew exclaims.

'No, no, my boy,' the other corrects. 'I'm no moralist. I'm just an observer of my fellows. They say that those who *watch* see the most of the game. Well, I'm an observer—and I've told you what I see.'

.   .   .   .   .

In the foregoing imaginary conversation we have brought to the reader's notice two exceedingly alarming modern tendencies, the tendency towards mass-produced personality and the tendency towards wholesale moral declension.

How are these two tendencies to be combated?

It is the author's view that Methodism constitutes a God-given weapon—all shining and ready for this very purpose! Right from its inception, Methodism has stressed both *the value of the individual soul in the sight of God*, and *the challenge of the Gospel message to personal responsibility*! Growing, as it did, in the early days of the Industrial Revolution, Methodism had to combat with all the resources at its disposal, the diabolical soul-destroying tendencies of that revolution, when men, women, and children tended to be looked upon and treated as mere 'hands' or industrial slaves, for the tending and operating of the great new machines. Against this background, original Methodism developed, with all the while Wesley and his roughrider preachers proclaiming (in and out of season) the Gospel of Individual Worth—the *value* of every soul to God, and the *obligations* of every soul to both its Maker and neighbour.

The social repercussions of these emphases were astounding! Directly and indirectly there followed in the ensuing two hundred years a veritable spate of humanitarian enterprises. Schools, orphanages, alms-houses, rescue homes, and other philanthropic enterprises of every description sprang into being. *Men mattered!* They were not mere cogs in the industrial machine; they were souls whom God loved and for whom Christ died. They were *individuals*, each of whom had, locked within his heart, amazing latent possibilities which, under the touch of Christ, could be released and developed. Men could be *born again*, they could in Christ become *new creations!* Thus, two hundred years ago, the grim tendencies of the Industrial Revolution to *de*humanize the masses and so exploit them was combated and arrested—*by Methodism!*

Once again the masses are in danger—not this time from the exploiting industrialists, but from the sinister power of modern inventions, particularly instruments of propaganda. Nothing is more needed than a counter-force to combat and arrest this tendency, a force which can turn the drift from mechanical conformity to indi-vidualistic nonconformity, from the tendency to submerge individuality in the mass or State, and give him back a sense of personal worth and personal responsibility—both to his God and his neighbour.

This, we believe, Methodism can do!

.   .   .   .   .

Now, the other alarming modern tendency which the uncle adumbrated in his conversation with his nephew was the tendency towards wholesale moral declension. How is this sinister trend to be combated and arrested?

Again, is not Methodism an ideal and ready-made

weapon? Is not Methodism's emphasis upon scriptural holiness the answer?

No one can read the literature of early Methodism without being impressed by the stress which is laid all the way through upon this important emphasis. Wesley himself said that his purpose was to 'spread scriptural holiness throughout the land'. That aim, expressed in a hundred different ways, permeates all the early Methodist utterances. In the rules of Wesley's preachers, collected and approved directly after his death in 1797, there appear statements like this: 'above all', the aim of Methodist preachers is 'to reform the nation, by spreading scriptural holiness throughout the land'. Then, in answer to the question, 'What was the rise of Methodism?' there appears this significant answer:

'In 1729 the late Mr. Wesley and his brother, upon reading the Bible, saw they could not be saved without holiness; they followed after it, and incited others to do the same. In 1737 they saw holiness come by faith. They saw, likewise, that men are justified before they are sanctified; but still holiness was the point. God then thrust them out, utterly against their will, to raise up a holy people.' Again, in answer to the question, 'How shall we try those who think they are moved by the Holy Ghost to preach the Gospel?' there comes the answer, 'Do they know God as a pardoning God? Have they the love of God abiding in them? Are they holy in all manner of conversation? etc.' Holiness was beyond question the central aim of early Methodism.

No doubt to modern ears this phrase 'scriptural holiness' sounds quaint and ultra-pious. When, however, one recalls all that has been said in the chapter on holiness—that it is nothing less than Christ-likeness—and when one remembers how those original Methodists fought with wondrous valiance against the evils of intemperance, impurity, gambling, social injustice, and the like—then one realizes how relevant to modern needs is this particular Methodist emphasis.

Here, then, is the antidote to the alarming modern spread of moral decay! Here is the much-needed check upon the prevalent moral rot!

At the church where the author is privileged to minister, there is a Fellowship of men which has in its ranks several works managers, schoolmasters, shopkeepers, and artisans. Each week these men meet for worship, fellowship, and mutual helpfulness. Here some of the difficulties of faith and life are talked over, and here problems are discussed and hearts unveiled. Then back the members go to their various walks in life. As the result of this Fellowship there are, we know, certain factory offices where the atmosphere is different from what it was a year or so ago, where 'standards' are higher and tempers more controlled. There are works dining-rooms where the daily conversations are richer, there are factory discussion groups where Christian idealism is ever to the fore and where a 'witness' for the faith is always sure to be made. There are homes where, as the result of the Fellowship, family prayers have been instituted, and so forth. The Fellowship is in no way unique. It is simply a 'cell' of live Christians. There are many such all over Methodism. But how unimaginably the whole life of this nation could be elevated and enriched and purified if such Fellowships were to become far, far more numerous! Thus, in a very short time, a healthy *nonconformity* and a healthy *holiness* could spread!

·　　·　　·　　·　　·

Are you, reader, a 'Methodist'? If so, are you familiar, as you ought to be, with the rich history of your denomination, and are you proud of it? Are you a Methodist local preacher? Do you in your preaching stress and iterate these great Methodist emphases which we have here outlined? Are you a Methodist Class Leader? If so, do you urge upon the members of your class the duty of personal discipline and stress the importance of 'scriptural holiness'?

But perhaps you are none of these! Maybe you are just a young person into whose hands this book has come more by accident than design. And perhaps the things of Christ—never mind the things of Methodism—mean little to you, at any rate from an *experimental* point of view! If so, may I address a final word to you? It is to repeat again, with renewed emphasis, the challenge which is contained in the end of each chapter—the challenge of one's personal responsibility in all the matters here discussed. Salvation is offered to you. It must be accepted in faith. You can *know* that you are saved—by the witness of God's Spirit within your heart; and by the evidence of a changed life—and that changed life must be a life of developing holiness.

Consider this final parable:

Some sixty odd years ago there lived in a Cornish village two young men who were bosom friends. They had been to school together, and now they worked together. Often they slept together. They were inseparable. The joy or the sorrow of each was shared by both. Then came a crisis—a *crisis of decision*. They had for some time been moral drifters—and they were drifting to danger! But one night their curiosity led them into an evangelistic meeting—and there they were unexpectedly faced with a great decision. They were offered the choice of two cups. On the one hand, the cup of sensuality. On the other, the cup of salvation. Both were freely and pointedly offered, and the two men deliberately chose. One took the former, the other the latter. The one who chose sensuality was soon liable to be caught in the clutches of the law, and to escape he fled to New Zealand, where eventually he fell into a drunkard's grave. The other chose salvation, and his life was transformed. He became a new creature in Christ Jesus. A great sense of purpose and direction came to him. He began to look around for opportunities of Christian service, and, to equip himself for such work, began to read and study. He became a tremendous influence for good. Holiness began to develop in his soul, and eventually he became a local preacher, in which capacity he served with wondrous effectiveness until illness laid him low. He brought up two children— two of the finest characters you could imagine. One is a brother minister.

Such a choice comes to every man at some time. On the WAY ONE CHOOSES everything depends.

Maybe my little book has brought you face to face with such a choice now. If so, it will have done something worth while; and if, as the result of this challenge, your life is changed, and holiness pervades your heart, and you become a flaming, eager 'Methodist' Christian —then, who can tell what such a life-change may mean, both to you and to your generation!

But *you* must choose!

> This is the time; no more delay!
> This is the acceptable day;
> Come in, this moment, at His call,
> *And live for Him* who died for all.

SUGGESTED BOOKS FOR FURTHER STUDY

The Life of John Wesley. JOHN TELFORD (Epworth Press).

The Knight of the Burning Heart. LESLIE F. CHURCH (Epworth Press).

Methodist Good Companions. G. ELSIE HARRISON (Epworth Press).

Wesley Veterans, Vols. 1 and 2 (Epworth Press). Out of print.

The Roots of Methodism. W. V. FITZGERALD (Epworth Press).

John Wesley and His Horse. T. FERRIER HULME (Epworth Press).

Wesley's England. J. H. WHITELEY (Epworth Press).

What Methodists Believe and Preach. HENRY BETT.

Methodism can be Born Again. W. E. SANGSTER (Hodder and Stoughton).

Wesley's Forty-four Sermons. New Edition, 1944 (Epworth Press).

Printed in Great Britain by
The Camelot Press Ltd., London and Southampton